Adult Coloring Book Animals of the World Volume I

Copyright © 2016

For resale and distribution information, please contact us via www.booboone.com

Elephant by Delarno

Male Lion

Alpaca by Lena London

Arctic Fox

Two Baby Goats

Bactrian Camel

Black Bear Sitting

Bobcat by Lena London

Bucking Horse

Bull Riding

Capybara by Lena London

Leopard

British Shorthair Cat

Cheetah

Chipmunk by Lena London

Common Brushtail Possum

Cute Bunny Rabbit

Deer

Desert Bighorn Sheep

Dingo (wild dog) by Lena London

Domestic Sheep

Donkey

Eastern-gray Squirrel by Lena London

Bucking Mustang

European Beaver

Flying Squirrel

Giant Panda Bear

Grizzly Bear

Grey Arabian Horse

Honey Badger

Hyena by Lena London

Kangaroo

Koala

Lar Gibbon

Lamb

Lioness Lena London

Lynx

Masai Giraffe

Meerkat by Lena London

Moose

Mountain Cottontail Rabbit

Mule Deer

Musk Ox by Natalia Moskovkina

Okapi by Lena London

Orangutan

Pig

Howling Wolf

Polar Bear

Porcupine by Lena London

Prairie-dog by Lena London

Snarling Tiger

Common Panda Family